PERFORMANCE ASSESSMENT TEACHER'S GUIDE

3

Cover and Title Page Photo Credit: ©imagewerks/Getty Images

Printed in the U.S.A.

ISBN 978-0-544-46521-3

8 9 10   0928   23 22 21 20 19 18 17 16

4500593825   A B C D E F G

Approaching Performance Assessments with Confidence

By Carol Jago

The best assessments reflect best practice. Rather than asking students to perform artificial tasks, assessments worth giving include texts worth reading and tasks worth doing. Ideally, time spent on such formative assessments shouldn't be time lost to instruction but rather an opportunity both for students to demonstrate what they have learned as well as a chance for additional practice.

Malcolm Gladwell estimates in his book *Outliers* that mastering a skill requires about 10,000 hours of dedicated practice. He argues that individuals who are outstanding in their field have one thing in common—many, many hours of working at it. Gladwell claims that success is less dependent on innate talent than it is on practice. Now I'm pretty sure that I could put in 10,000 hours at a ballet studio and still be a terrible dancer, but I agree with Gladwell that, "Practice isn't the thing you do once you're good. It's the thing you do that makes you good."

Not just any kind of practice will help students master performance assessments, though. Effective practice needs to focus on improvement. That is why this series of reading and writing tasks begins with a model of the kind of reading and writing students are working towards, then takes them through practice exercises, and finally invites them to perform the skills they have practiced.

Once through the cycle is only the beginning. You will want your students to repeat the process several times over until close reading, supporting claims with evidence, and crafting a compelling essay is something they approach with confidence. Notice that I didn't say "with ease." I wish it were otherwise, but in my experience as a teacher and as an author, writing well is never easy.

I hope you find these assessment tools a valuable, seamless addition to your curriculum.

v

Unit 3 Response to Literature

Animal Tricksters

Unit 4 Narrative

Strange Situations

Unit 5 Mixed Practice

On Your Own

All About Pets

STEP 1 ANALYZE THE MODEL

Should people keep birds as pets?

Page 5
Discuss and Decide

As students discuss why birds can get bored in cages, remind them to cite textual evidence.

Page 7
Close Read

Student answers should demonstrate comprehension and draw evidence from the text. They may cite that birds are colorful, funny, smart, or can be trained.

Page 9
Discuss and Decide

As students discuss whether people should keep birds as pets, remind them to cite textual evidence.

Page 11
Discuss and Decide

As students discuss whether or not they are convinced by Eddie's essay, remind them to cite textual evidence.

Page 12
Be Clear!

Accept reasonable sentences that demonstrate clarification of Eddie's ideas.

STEP 2 PRACTICE THE TASK

Should pets be allowed in school?

Page 15
Discuss and Decide

As students discuss two things that Dr. Hoffman learned from animals, remind them to cite textual evidence.

Page 17
Close Read

Student answers should demonstrate comprehension and draw evidence from the text. They may explain that although others may worry that dogs are not clean, Cocoa is not very messy.

© Houghton Mifflin Harcourt Publishing Company

Page 19
Discuss and Decide

As students discuss why it's important for students to wash their hands after handling an animal, remind them to cite textual evidence.

Page 21
Close Read

Student answers should demonstrate comprehension and draw evidence from the text. They may cite that *salmonella* outbreaks seem to be increasing. They may also explain that although the ten-year outbreak total seems low, the chart does not tell us how many people were affected in each outbreak.

Pages 22–23
Respond to Questions

1. Accept responses that demonstrate comprehension and draw evidence from each source. The parent and student letters agree that pets should be allowed in school, and the infographic does not agree. The pet policy can be used to support either position.

2. Prose Constructed-Response

Scoring Notes: Use the rubric to evaluate student responses. Responses may include but are not limited to:

• The reasons given in either of the letters.

• The rules in the pet policy that support this position.

2	The response gives sufficient evidence of the ability to cite reasons that support opinions and/or ideas.
1	The response gives limited evidence of the ability to cite reasons that support opinions and/or ideas.
0	The response provides no evidence of the ability to cite reasons that support opinions and/or ideas.

3. Prose Constructed-Response

Scoring Notes: Use the rubric to evaluate student responses. Responses may include but are not limited to:

• The supporting details and data in the infographic.

• The rules in the pet policy that support this position.

2	The response gives sufficient evidence of the ability to cite reasons that support opinions and/or ideas.
1	The response gives limited evidence of the ability to cite reasons that support opinions and/or ideas.
0	The response provides no evidence of the ability to cite reasons that support opinions and/or ideas.

Pages 24–25
Planning and Prewriting
Review and critique students' planning documents; offer feedback as needed.

Pages 26–28
Opinion Essay
Scoring Notes: Use the rubric to evaluate student responses.

	Development of Ideas	Organization	Clarity of Language	Language and Conventions
4	The response addresses the prompt and shows effective and comprehensive development of the opinion using text-based evidence, clear and convincing reasoning, and/or description.	The response demonstrates coherence and clarity, a logical organization that includes an introduction and conclusion, and a logical progression of ideas.	The response establishes and maintains an effective style, including precise language, descriptive words and phrases, connecting words and phrases, and academic vocabulary.	The response demonstrates a command of standard English conventions consistent with effectively edited writing.
3	The response addresses the prompt and shows effective development of the topic using text-based evidence, reasoning, and/or description.	The response demonstrates some logical organization and includes an introduction and conclusion.	Some descriptive words, as well as some connecting words and phrases, are used to express ideas with clarity.	The response demonstrates a command of standard English conventions, although there may be some minor errors in grammar and usage.

	Development of Ideas	Organization	Clarity of Language	Language and Conventions
2	The response addresses the prompt and shows some development of the topic but fails to use text-based evidence, reasoning, and/or description.	The response demonstrates little logical organization and includes either an introduction or a conclusion.	Few descriptive words, as well as a few connecting words and phrases, are used and ideas are not expressed as clearly as possible.	The response demonstrates a command of standard English conventions, although there are major errors in grammar and usage.
1	The response does not directly address the prompt, shows no development of the topic, and fails to use text-based evidence, reasoning, and/or description.	The response demonstrates little logical organization and fails to include either an introduction or a conclusion.	No descriptive words or connecting words and phrases are used and ideas are not expressed with clarity.	Errors in grammar and usage create confusion of meaning.
0	The response demonstrates no evidence of the ability to write an opinion essay.			

STEP 3 PERFORM THE TASK

Which are better: cats or dogs?

Page 31
Close Read

Student answers should demonstrate comprehension and draw evidence from the text. They may cite details from Henry's description of "man's best friend."

Page 33
Close Read

Student answers should demonstrate comprehension and draw evidence from the text. They may cite details from Juliette's description of her cat, Rascal.

Page 35
Discuss and Decide

As students discuss one way that cats are different than dogs, remind them to cite textual evidence.

Page 36

Discuss and Decide

As students discuss the details that suggest that dogs are more popular than cats, remind them to cite textual evidence.

Pages 37–38

Respond to Questions

1. d.

2. a.

3. c.

4. c.

5. Accept responses that demonstrate comprehension and draw evidence from the source. The letter from Henry and the chart agree that dogs are better than cats, and the letter from Juliette supports the position that cats are better than dogs. The fact sheet can be used to support either position.

6. Prose Constructed-Response

Scoring Notes: Use the rubric to evaluate student responses. Responses may include but are not limited to:

• Factual information from "Data About Dogs."

• Examples from "Data About Dogs."

2	The response gives sufficient evidence of the ability to cite reasons that support opinions and/or ideas.
1	The response gives limited evidence of the ability to cite reasons that support opinions and/or ideas.
0	The response provides no evidence of the ability to cite reasons that support opinions and/or ideas.

Pages 39–40
Opinion Essay

Scoring Notes: Use the rubric to evaluate student responses.

	Development of Ideas	Organization	Clarity of Language	Language and Conventions
4	The response addresses the prompt and shows effective and comprehensive development of the opinion using text-based evidence, clear and convincing reasoning, and/or description.	The response demonstrates coherence and clarity, a logical organization that includes an introduction and conclusion, and a logical progression of ideas.	The response establishes and maintains an effective style, including precise language, descriptive words and phrases, connecting words and phrases, and academic vocabulary.	The response demonstrates a command of standard English conventions consistent with effectively edited writing.
3	The response addresses the prompt and shows effective development of the topic using text-based evidence, reasoning, and/or description.	The response demonstrates some logical organization and includes an introduction and conclusion.	Some descriptive words, as well as some connecting words and phrases, are used to express ideas with clarity.	The response demonstrates a command of standard English conventions, although there may be some minor errors in grammar and usage.
2	The response addresses the prompt and shows some development of the topic but fails to use text-based evidence, reasoning, and/or description.	The response demonstrates little logical organization and includes either an introduction or a conclusion.	Few descriptive words, as well as a few connecting words and phrases, are used and ideas are not expressed as clearly as possible.	The response demonstrates a command of standard English conventions, although there are major errors in grammar and usage.

	Development of Ideas	Organization	Clarity of Language	Language and Conventions
1	The response does not directly address the prompt, shows no development of the topic, and fails to use text-based evidence, reasoning, and/or description.	The response demonstrates little logical organization and fails to include either an introduction or a conclusion.	No descriptive words or connecting words and phrases are used and ideas are not expressed with clarity.	Errors in grammar and usage create confusion of meaning.
0	The response demonstrates no evidence of the ability to write an opinion essay.			

250 Years Ago

STEP 1 ANALYZE THE MODEL

How did American Indians' surroundings affect the way they lived?

Page 47
Discuss and Decide

As students explain the difference between what the Desert Indians and the Plains Indians ate, remind them to cite textual evidence.

Page 51
Close Read

Student answers should demonstrate comprehension and draw evidence from the text. They may cite that the Plains Indians were nomadic and traveled place to place while hunting buffalo, and that their teepees were easy to set up and move.

Page 53
Discuss and Decide

As students locate two examples where Seiji included details from both sources in a single paragraph, remind them to cite textual evidence.

Page 54
Organizing an Informative Essay

Accept reasonable sentences that demonstrate understanding of Seiji's cause-and-effect informative essay, and the logical sequencing of his ideas.

STEP 2 PRACTICE THE TASK

How did colonists travel in America?

Page 59
Close Read

Student answers should demonstrate comprehension and draw evidence from the text. They may cite that travel in the eighteenth century always took a lot of time. Travel was unsafe and tiring if you walked, expensive and rough going if you traveled by horse, very uncomfortable if you traveled by carriage, and limited by water access if you traveled by boat.

Page 63

Discuss and Decide

As students discuss the advantages and disadvantages of taking a ferry rather than riding a horse, remind them to cite textual evidence.

Pages 64–65

Respond to Questions

1. c.

2. b.

3. a.

4. c.

5. Prose Constructed-Response

Scoring Notes: Use the rubric to evaluate student responses. Responses may include but are not limited to:

- Evidence that horses made travel in eighteenth-century America much easier than walking.

- Evidence that horses required significant money to purchase, and had to travel the same rough terrain as those traveling on foot.

2	The response gives sufficient evidence of the ability to cite details and evidence to support ideas.
1	The response gives limited evidence of the ability to cite details and evidence to support ideas.
0	The response provides no evidence of the ability to cite details and evidence to support ideas.

6. Prose Constructed-Response

Scoring Notes: Use the rubric to evaluate student responses. Responses may include but are not limited to:

- Evidence from either or both sources showing that travel in colonial America took a very long time.

- Evidence from either or both sources showing that roads and ferries were rough going, and sometimes dangerous.

2	The response gives sufficient evidence of the ability to cite details and evidence to support ideas.
1	The response gives limited evidence of the ability to cite details and evidence to support ideas.
0	The response provides no evidence of the ability to cite details and evidence to support opinions and/or ideas.

Pages 66–67
Planning and Prewriting

Review and critique students' planning documents; offer feedback as needed.

Pages 68–70
Informative Essay

Scoring Notes: Use the rubric to evaluate student essays.

	Development of Ideas	Organization	Clarity of Language	Language and Conventions
4	The response addresses the prompt and shows effective and comprehensive development of the controlling idea using text-based evidence, clear and convincing reasoning, and/or description.	The response demonstrates coherence and clarity, a logical organization that includes an introduction and conclusion, and a logical progression of ideas.	The response establishes and maintains an effective style, including precise language, descriptive words and phrases, connecting words and phrases, and academic vocabulary.	The response demonstrates a command of standard English conventions consistent with effectively edited writing.
3	The response addresses the prompt and shows effective development of the topic using text-based evidence, reasoning, and/or description.	The response demonstrates some logical organization and includes an introduction and conclusion.	Some descriptive words, as well as some connecting words and phrases, are used to express ideas with clarity.	The response demonstrates a command of standard English conventions, although there may be some minor errors in grammar and usage.

	Development of Ideas	Organization	Clarity of Language	Language and Conventions
2	The response addresses the prompt and shows some development of the topic but fails to use text-based evidence, reasoning, and/or description.	The response demonstrates little logical organization and includes either an introduction or a conclusion.	Few descriptive words, as well as a few connecting words and phrases, are used and ideas are not expressed as clearly as possible.	The response demonstrates a command of standard English conventions, although there are major errors in grammar and usage.
1	The response does not directly address the prompt, shows no development of the topic, and fails to use text-based evidence, reasoning, and/or description.	The response demonstrates little logical organization and fails to include either an introduction or a conclusion.	No descriptive words or connecting words and phrases are used and ideas are not expressed with clarity.	Errors in grammar and usage create confusion of meaning.
0	The response demonstrates no evidence of the ability to write an informative essay.			

STEP 3 PERFORM THE TASK

What was everyday life like for children in colonial America?

Page 73
Close Read

Student answers should demonstrate comprehension and draw evidence from the text. They may cite details from the paragraphs that describe the blacksmith family, the farming family, the girls' chores, or the younger kids' chores.

Page 75
Discuss and Decide

As students discuss the main subjects that colonial children studied in school, remind them to cite textual evidence.

Page 78
Discuss and Decide

As students discuss the differences between dolls of today and the dolls of 250 years ago, remind them to cite textual evidence.

Respond to Questions

1. c.

2. a.

3. d.

4. a.

5. Prose Constructed-Response

Scoring Notes: Use the rubric to evaluate student responses. Responses may include but are not limited to:

- Evidence that some boys might go on to other schools.

- Evidence that many boys would become apprentices to learn the family trade.

2	The response gives sufficient evidence of the ability to cite details and evidence to support ideas.
1	The response gives limited evidence of the ability to cite details and evidence to support ideas.
0	The response provides no evidence of the ability to cite details and evidence to support ideas.

6. Prose Constructed-Response

Scoring Notes: Use the rubric to evaluate student responses. Responses may include but are not limited to:

- Evidence that Source 1 really doesn't discuss what kids did for fun in colonial times. It does mention that kids played games to make the time pass while they worked.

- Evidence that Source 2 doesn't talk about kids having fun at all.

- Evidence that Source 3 gives the best understanding of what colonial kids did for fun. It tells us the names of the games, gives descriptions, and tells how they were played.

2	The response gives sufficient evidence of the ability to cite details and evidence to support ideas.
1	The response gives limited evidence of the ability to cite details and evidence to support ideas.
0	The response provides no evidence of the ability to cite details and evidence to support ideas.

Pages 81–82
Informative Essay
Scoring Notes: Use the rubric to evaluate student responses.

	Development of Ideas	Organization	Clarity of Language	Language and Conventions
4	The response addresses the prompt and shows effective and comprehensive development of the controlling idea using text-based evidence, clear and convincing reasoning, and/or description.	The response demonstrates coherence and clarity, a logical organization that includes an introduction and conclusion, and a logical progression of ideas.	The response establishes and maintains an effective style, including precise language, descriptive words and phrases, connecting words and phrases, and academic vocabulary.	The response demonstrates a command of standard English conventions consistent with effectively edited writing.
3	The response addresses the prompt and shows effective development of the topic using text-based evidence, reasoning, and/or description.	The response demonstrates some logical organization and includes an introduction and conclusion.	Some descriptive words, as well as some connecting words and phrases, are used to express ideas with clarity.	The response demonstrates a command of standard English conventions, although there may be some minor errors in grammar and usage.
2	The response addresses the prompt and shows some development of the topic but fails to use text-based evidence, reasoning, and/or description.	The response demonstrates little logical organization and includes either an introduction or a conclusion.	Few descriptive words, as well as a few connecting words and phrases, are used and ideas are not expressed as clearly as possible.	The response demonstrates a command of standard English conventions, although there are major errors in grammar and usage.

18

© Houghton Mifflin Harcourt Publishing Company

	Development of Ideas	Organization	Clarity of Language	Language and Conventions
1	The response does not directly address the prompt, shows no development of the topic, and fails to use text-based evidence, reasoning, and/or description.	The response demonstrates little logical organization and fails to include either an introduction or a conclusion.	No descriptive words or connecting words and phrases are used and ideas are not expressed with clarity.	Errors in grammar and usage create confusion of meaning.
0	The response demonstrates no evidence of the ability to write an informative essay.			

Animal Tricksters

STEP 1 ANALYZE THE MODEL

How do a character's actions drive the events of a story?

Page 87
Discuss and Decide

As students discuss what Grandma Spider asks Anansi to do, remind them to cite textual evidence.

Page 89
Discuss and Decide

As students discuss what Anansi's actions tell them about his character, remind them to cite textual evidence.

Page 91
Discuss and Decide

As students discuss why Anansi doesn't open the door for his neighbors right away, remind them to cite textual evidence.

Page 93
Discuss and Decide

As students discuss what happens to Anansi because he was afraid of getting caught, remind them to cite textual evidence.

Page 95
Discuss and Decide

As students discuss Molly's response to literature, remind them to cite textual evidence.

Page 96
Responding to Literature

Accept reasonable examples that demonstrate understanding of a character's actions and how they affect the story's events.

STEP 2 PRACTICE THE TASK

How does a trickster get what he wants?

Page 99
Discuss and Decide

As students discuss who the trickster is in this story, remind them to cite textual evidence.

Respond to Questions

1. d.

2. b.

3. a.

4. Prose Constructed-Response

   Scoring Notes: Use the rubric to evaluate student responses. Responses may include but are not limited to:

   • At first the Crow is suspicious.

   • Then she forgets her suspicion.

   • Then she is flattered.

2	The response gives sufficient evidence of the ability to gather, analyze, and integrate information within a source.
1	The response gives limited evidence of the ability to gather, analyze, and integrate information within a source.
0	The response provides no evidence of the ability to gather, analyze, and integrate information within a source.

5. Prose Constructed-Response

   Scoring Notes: Use the rubric to evaluate student responses. Responses may include but are not limited to:

   • The fact that Crow drops the cheese while sitting in the tree allows the Fox to catch it as it falls.

   • The Crow would be unable to get the cheese back from the Fox once he eats it.

2	The response gives sufficient evidence of the ability to gather, analyze, and integrate information within a source.
1	The response gives limited evidence of the ability to gather, analyze, and integrate information within a source.
0	The response provides no evidence of the ability to gather, analyze, and integrate information within a source.

6. Prose Constructed-Response

Scoring Notes: Use the rubric to evaluate student responses. Responses may include but are not limited to:

- Don't believe everything you hear.

- Flattery may trick a listener.

- A trickster succeeds only if his or her subject falls for the trick.

2	The response gives sufficient evidence of the ability to gather, analyze, and integrate information within a source.
1	The response gives limited evidence of the ability to gather, analyze, and integrate information within a source.
0	The response provides no evidence of the ability to gather, analyze, and integrate information within a source.

Pages 102–103
Planning and Prewriting

Review and critique students' planning charts; offer feedback as needed.

Pages 104–105
Response to Literature

Scoring Notes: Use the rubric to evaluate student responses.

	Development of Ideas	Organization	Clarity of Language	Language and Conventions
4	The response addresses the prompt and shows effective and comprehensive development of the controlling idea using text-based evidence, clear and convincing reasoning, and/or description.	The response demonstrates coherence and clarity, a logical organization that includes an introduction and conclusion, and a logical progression of ideas.	The response establishes and maintains an effective style, including precise language, descriptive words and phrases, connecting words and phrases, and academic vocabulary.	The response demonstrates a command of standard English conventions consistent with effectively edited writing.

	Development of Ideas	Organization	Clarity of Language	Language and Conventions
3	The response addresses the prompt and shows effective development of the topic using text-based evidence, reasoning, and/or description.	The response demonstrates some logical organization and includes an introduction and conclusion.	Some descriptive words, as well as some connecting words and phrases, are used to express ideas with clarity.	The response demonstrates a command of standard English conventions, although there may be some minor errors in grammar and usage.
2	The response addresses the prompt and shows some development of the topic but fails to use text-based evidence, reasoning, and/or description.	The response demonstrates little logical organization and includes either an introduction or a conclusion.	Few descriptive words, as well as a few connecting words and phrases, are used and ideas are not expressed as clearly as possible.	The response demonstrates a command of standard English conventions, although there are major errors in grammar and usage.
1	The response does not directly address the prompt, shows no development of the topic, and fails to use text-based evidence, reasoning, and/or description.	The response demonstrates little logical organization and fails to include either an introduction or a conclusion.	No descriptive words or connecting words and phrases are used and ideas are not expressed with clarity.	Errors in grammar and usage create confusion of meaning.
0	The response demonstrates no evidence of the ability to write a response to literature.			

STEP 3 PERFORM THE TASK

What are the character traits of a trickster?

Page 109

Close Read

Student answers should demonstrate comprehension and draw evidence from the text. They may cite that Turtle's pond has "everything any turtle could ever want," including alder trees with shade, a grassy bank for sunning, and plenty of fish to eat.

Page 111
Close Read

Student answers should demonstrate comprehension and draw evidence from the text. They may cite that Beaver believes the pond is his; that he has cut down the trees, built the dam, and made the pond nice and deep.

Page 113
Discuss and Decide

As students discuss why Beaver agrees to race Turtle, remind them to cite textual evidence.

Page 114
Discuss and Decide

As students discuss how turtle's situation at the end of the story is similar to his situation at the beginning, remind them to cite textual evidence.

Pages 115–116
Respond to Questions

1. d.

2. d.

3. a.

4. c.

5. Prose Constructed-Response

Scoring Notes: Use the rubric to evaluate student responses. Responses may include but are not limited to:

- Turtle's pond has "everything any turtle could ever want."

- Turtle likes the fact that his pond has alder trees with shade, a grassy bank for sunning, and plenty of fish to eat.

2	The response gives sufficient evidence of the ability to gather, analyze, and integrate information within a source.
1	The response gives limited evidence of the ability to gather, analyze, and integrate information within a source.
0	The response provides no evidence of the ability to gather, analyze, and integrate information within a source.

6. Prose Constructed-Response

Scoring Notes: Use the rubric to evaluate student responses. Responses may include but are not limited to:

- Turtle swims up to Beaver during the contest and latches onto Beaver's tail with his teeth.

- Shaking his tail back and forth, Beaver swings Turtle onto the bank of the pond.

- Beaver was too busy trying to swim, and did not see Turtle until Turtle was on the bank.

2	The response gives sufficient evidence of the ability to gather, analyze, and integrate information within a source.
1	The response gives limited evidence of the ability to gather, analyze, and integrate information within a source.
0	The response provides no evidence of the ability to gather, analyze, and integrate information within a source.

7. Prose Constructed-Response

Scoring Notes: Use the rubric to evaluate student responses. Responses may include but are not limited to:

- The pond changes after Beaver builds his dam.

- The pond is much larger and deeper, the trees have been cut down, and the grassy bank is underwater.

- Once Turtle wins the race, the setting is restored to how it was at the beginning of the story.

2	The response gives sufficient evidence of the ability to gather, analyze, and integrate information within a source.
1	The response gives limited evidence of the ability to gather, analyze, and integrate information within a source.
0	The response provides no evidence of the ability to gather, analyze, and integrate information within a source.

Scoring Notes: Use the rubric to evaluate student responses.

	Development of Ideas	Organization	Clarity of Language	Language and Conventions
4	The response addresses the prompt and shows effective and comprehensive development of the controlling idea using text-based evidence, clear and convincing reasoning, and/or description.	The response demonstrates coherence and clarity, a logical organization that includes an introduction and conclusion, and a logical progression of ideas.	The response establishes and maintains an effective style, including precise language, descriptive words and phrases, connecting words and phrases, and domain-specific vocabulary.	The response demonstrates a command of standard English conventions consistent with effectively edited writing.
3	The response addresses the prompt and shows effective development of the topic using text-based evidence, reasoning, and/or description.	The response demonstrates some logical organization and includes an introduction and conclusion.	Some descriptive words, as well as some connecting words and phrases, are used to express ideas with clarity.	The response demonstrates a command of standard English conventions, although there may be some minor errors in grammar and usage.
2	The response addresses the prompt and shows some development of the topic but fails to use text-based evidence, reasoning, and/or description.	The response demonstrates little logical organization and includes either an introduction or a conclusion.	Few descriptive words, as well as a few connecting words and phrases, are used and ideas are not expressed as clearly as possible.	The response demonstrates a command of standard English conventions, although there are major errors in grammar and usage.

	Development of Ideas	Organization	Clarity of Language	Language and Conventions
1	The response does not directly address the prompt, shows no development of the topic, and fails to use text-based evidence, reasoning, and/or description.	The response demonstrates little logical organization and fails to include either an introduction or a conclusion.	No descriptive words or connecting words and phrases are used and ideas are not expressed with clarity.	Errors in grammar and usage create confusion of meaning.
0	The response demonstrates no evidence of the ability to write a response to literature.			

Strange Situations

STEP 1 ANALYZE THE MODEL

What happens when cell phones don't work?

Page 125
Close Read

Student answers should demonstrate comprehension and draw evidence from the text. They may cite that landlines are connected by cable, and cell phone connections take place through radio waves. They may also cite that cell phones very often do not work underground, and may not be used in places where they could interfere with other machines or electronics.

Page 127
Discuss and Decide

As students discuss how Adrien includes information from the sources to make his narrative believable, remind them to cite textual evidence.

Page 128
Set the Scene!

Accept reasonable sentences that demonstrate understanding of the different settings that Adrien uses in his narrative, and how the development of one setting description could strengthen his narrative.

STEP 2 PRACTICE THE TASK

What happens when an ostrich visits your house?

Page 133
Close Read

Student answers will vary, but they should demonstrate comprehension and draw evidence from the text. Students may cite that an ostrich might be too tall for the apartment shown, that it might not have enough room to roam, or that it might get hurt if it tried to run. Students may also cite that an ostrich would look for a place to hide if it got scared, food when it got hungry, and that it would make a mess.

Pages 134–135
Respond to Questions

1. d.

2. b.

3. a.

4. Prose Constructed-Response

Scoring Notes: Use the rubric to evaluate student responses. Responses may include but are not limited to:

- Evidence that the ostrich would be used to more room than a human dwelling would provide, and it might get scared.

- Evidence that the ostrich would bump into things if it were too big or if it tried to run fast.

- Evidence that the ostrich would try to defend itself, and it might get hurt.

- Evidence that the ostrich would become hungry if it couldn't find the right food.

2	The response gives sufficient evidence of the ability to utilize factual information from multiple sources to support a narrative.
1	The response gives limited evidence of the ability to utilize factual information from multiple sources to support a narrative.
0	The response gives no evidence of the ability to support a narrative with factual information from multiple sources.

5. Prose Constructed-Response

Scoring Notes: Use the rubric to evaluate student responses. Responses may include but are not limited to:

- Evidence that the ostrich would like the kitchen, because it could find food.

- Evidence that the ostrich would like the bathroom, because it could hide in the bathtub.

- Evidence that the ostrich would like the living room, because it would have the most room there.

2	The response gives sufficient evidence of the ability to utilize factual information from multiple sources to support a narrative.
1	The response gives limited evidence of the ability to utilize factual information from multiple sources to support a narrative.
0	The response gives no evidence of the ability to support a narrative with factual information from multiple sources.

6. Prose Constructed-Response

Scoring Notes: Use the rubric to evaluate student responses. Responses may include but are not limited to:

- Evidence that ostriches are big and tall.
- Evidence that ostriches have a lot of room to roam on the African savanna.
- Evidence that ostriches likes to run.
- Evidence that ostriches sometimes need to hide.

2	The response gives sufficient evidence of the ability to utilize factual information from multiple sources to support a narrative.
1	The response gives limited evidence of the ability to utilize factual information from multiple sources to support a narrative.
0	The response gives no evidence of the ability to support a narrative with factual information from multiple sources.

Pages 136–137
Planning and Prewriting

Review and critique students' planning charts; offer feedback as needed.

Pages 138–139
Narrative

Scoring Notes: Use the rubric to evaluate student responses.

	Development of Ideas	Organization	Clarity of Language	Language and Conventions
4	The response addresses the prompt and effectively establishes a narrator, setting, and characters.	The response demonstrates coherence and clarity, a logical organization that includes an introduction and conclusion, and a logical progression of ideas.	The response establishes and maintains an effective style, including precise language, descriptive words and phrases, connecting words and phrases, and dialogue.	The response demonstrates a command of standard English conventions consistent with effectively edited writing.

© Houghton Mifflin Harcourt Publishing Company

	Development of Ideas	Organization	Clarity of Language	Language and Conventions
3	The response addresses the prompt and adequately establishes a narrator, setting, and characters.	The response demonstrates some logical organization and includes an introduction and conclusion.	Some descriptive words, as well as some connecting words and phrases, are used to express ideas with clarity.	The response demonstrates a command of standard English conventions, although there may be some minor errors in grammar and usage.
2	The response addresses the prompt, but inconsistently establishes a narrator, setting, and characters.	The response demonstrates little logical organization and includes either an introduction or a conclusion.	Few descriptive words and few connecting words and phrases are used, and ideas are not expressed as clearly as possible.	The response demonstrates a command of standard English conventions, although there are major errors in grammar and usage.
1	The response does not directly address the prompt, and does not establish a narrator, setting, or characters.	The response demonstrates little logical organization and fails to include either an introduction or a conclusion.	No descriptive words or connecting words or phrases are used, and ideas are not expressed with clarity.	Errors in grammar and usage create confusion of meaning.
0	The response demonstrates no evidence of the ability to write a narrative.			

STEP 3 PERFORM THE TASK

What happens when you develop an animal's abilities?

Page 145
Close Read

Student answers will vary, but they should demonstrate comprehension and draw evidence from the text.

Pages 146–148

1. c.

2. a.

3. a.

4. d.

5. Prose Constructed-Response

Scoring Notes: Use the rubric to evaluate student responses. Responses may include but are not limited to:

- The fact that the sperm whale can hold its breath for up to 90 minutes.

- The fact that the longest a human has ever been able to hold his or her breath is 22 minutes.

2	The response gives sufficient evidence of the ability to utilize factual information from multiple sources to support a narrative.
1	The response gives limited evidence of the ability to utilize factual information from multiple sources to support a narrative.
0	The response gives no evidence of the ability to support a narrative with factual information from multiple sources.

6. Prose Constructed-Response

Scoring Notes: Use the rubric to evaluate student responses. Responses may include but are not limited to:

- Evidence from the Source 2 infographic that presents the African Elephant as the largest land animal on Earth.

- Evidence of the African Elephant's size.

2	The response gives sufficient evidence of the ability to utilize factual information from multiple sources to support a narrative.
1	The response gives limited evidence of the ability to utilize factual information from multiple sources to support a narrative.
0	The response gives no evidence of the ability to support a narrative with factual information from multiple sources.

7. Prose Constructed-Response

Scoring Notes: Use the rubric to evaluate student responses. Responses may include but are not limited to:

- Evidence that bats use echolocation as they fly. Bats send out sound waves that hit objects and bounce back to the bat. Because bats can "see" using sound, they can tell where objects are without the need for light.

- Evidence that cats have the ability to see in almost complete darkness.

2	The response gives sufficient evidence of the ability to utilize factual information from multiple sources to support a narrative.
1	The response gives limited evidence of the ability to utilize factual information from multiple sources to support a narrative.
0	The response gives no evidence of the ability to support a narrative with factual information from multiple sources.

Pages 149–150

Narrative

Scoring Notes: Use the rubric to evaluate student responses.

	Development of Ideas	Organization	Clarity of Language	Language and Conventions
4	The response addresses the prompt and effectively establishes a narrator, setting, and characters.	The response demonstrates coherence and clarity, a logical organization that includes an introduction and conclusion, and a logical progression of ideas.	The response establishes and maintains an effective style, including precise language, descriptive words and phrases, connecting words and phrases, and dialogue.	The response demonstrates a command of standard English conventions consistent with effectively edited writing.

	Development of Ideas	Organization	Clarity of Language	Language and Conventions
3	The response addresses the prompt and adequately establishes a narrator, setting, and characters.	The response demonstrates some logical organization and includes an introduction and conclusion.	Some descriptive words, as well as some connecting words and phrases, are used to express ideas with clarity.	The response demonstrates a command of standard English conventions, although there may be some minor errors in grammar and usage.
2	The response addresses the prompt, but inconsistently establishes a narrator, setting, and characters.	The response demonstrates little logical organization and includes either an introduction or a conclusion.	Few descriptive words and few connecting words and phrases are used, and ideas are not expressed as clearly as possible.	The response demonstrates a command of standard English conventions, although there are major errors in grammar and usage.
1	The response does not directly address the prompt, and does not establish a narrator, setting, or characters.	The response demonstrates little logical organization and fails to include either an introduction or a conclusion.	No descriptive words or connecting words or phrases are used, and ideas are not expressed with clarity.	Errors in grammar and usage create confusion of meaning.
0	The response demonstrates no evidence of the ability to write a narrative.			

On Your Own

TASK 1 OPINION ESSAY

Page 161

1. b.

2. Prose Constructed-Response

Scoring Notes: Use the rubric to evaluate student responses. Responses may include but are not limited to:

- Evidence that chores teach children discipline and responsibility.

- Evidence that chores prepare young people for adulthood, teaching them that there are things we need to do, whether we like to or not.

2	The response gives sufficient evidence of the ability to cite reasons that support opinions and/or ideas.
1	The response gives limited evidence of the ability to cite reasons that support opinions and/or ideas.
0	The response provides no evidence of the ability to cite reasons that support opinions and/or ideas.

3. Prose Constructed-Response

Scoring Notes: Use the rubric to evaluate student responses. Responses may include but are not limited to:

- Evidence that children already have enough responsibility and that their days are full.

- Evidence that children are only young once, and they should be able to enjoy their free time.

- Evidence that chores are an adult responsibility.

- Evidence that children are unable to do all of the chores at home.

2	The response gives sufficient evidence of the ability to cite reasons that support opinions and/or ideas.
1	The response gives limited evidence of the ability to cite reasons that support opinions and/or ideas.
0	The response provides no evidence of the ability to cite reasons that support opinions and/or ideas.

Opinion Essay

Scoring Notes: Use the rubric to evaluate student responses.

	Development of Ideas	Organization	Clarity of Language	Language and Conventions
4	The response addresses the prompt and shows effective and comprehensive development of the opinion using text-based evidence, clear and convincing reasoning, and/or description.	The response demonstrates coherence and clarity, a logical organization that includes an introduction and conclusion, and a logical progression of ideas.	The response establishes and maintains an effective style, including precise language, descriptive words and phrases, connecting words and phrases, and academic vocabulary.	The response demonstrates a command of standard English conventions consistent with effectively edited writing.
3	The response addresses the prompt and shows effective development of the topic using text-based evidence, reasoning, and/or description.	The response demonstrates some logical organization and includes an introduction and conclusion.	Some descriptive words, as well as some connecting words and phrases, are used to express ideas with clarity.	The response demonstrates a command of standard English conventions, although there may be some minor errors in grammar and usage.
2	The response addresses the prompt and shows some development of the topic but fails to use text-based evidence, reasoning, and/or description.	The response demonstrates little logical organization and includes either an introduction or a conclusion.	Few descriptive words, as well as a few connecting words and phrases, are used and ideas are not expressed as clearly as possible.	The response demonstrates a command of standard English conventions, although there are major errors in grammar and usage.

	Development of Ideas	Organization	Clarity of Language	Language and Conventions
1	The response does not directly address the prompt, shows no development of the topic, and fails to use text-based evidence, reasoning, and/or description.	The response demonstrates little logical organization and fails to include either an introduction or a conclusion.	No descriptive words or connecting words and phrases are used and ideas are not expressed with clarity.	Errors in grammar and usage create confusion of meaning.
0	The response demonstrates no evidence of the ability to write an opinion essay.			

TASK 2 INFORMATIVE ESSAY

Page 171

1. a.

2. c.

3. b.

4. c.

Informative Essay

Scoring Notes: Use the rubric to evaluate student responses.

	Development of Ideas	Organization	Clarity of Language	Language and Conventions
4	The response addresses the prompt and shows effective and comprehensive development of the controlling idea using text-based evidence, clear and convincing reasoning, and/or description.	The response demonstrates coherence and clarity, a logical organization that includes an introduction and conclusion, and a logical progression of ideas.	The response establishes and maintains an effective style, including precise language, descriptive words and phrases, connecting words and phrases, and academic vocabulary.	The response demonstrates a command of standard English conventions consistent with effectively edited writing.
3	The response addresses the prompt and shows effective development of the topic using text-based evidence, reasoning, and/or description.	The response demonstrates some logical organization and includes an introduction and conclusion.	Some descriptive words, as well as some connecting words and phrases, are used to express ideas with clarity.	The response demonstrates a command of standard English conventions, although there may be some minor errors in grammar and usage.
2	The response addresses the prompt and shows some development of the topic but fails to use text-based evidence, reasoning, and/or description.	The response demonstrates little logical organization and includes either an introduction or a conclusion.	Few descriptive words, as well as a few connecting words and phrases, are used and ideas are not expressed as clearly as possible.	The response demonstrates a command of standard English conventions, although there are major errors in grammar and usage.

1	The response does not directly address the prompt. shows no development of the topic, and fails to use text-based evidence, reasoning, and/or description.	The response demonstrates little logical organization and fails to include either an introduction or a conclusion.	No descriptive words or connecting words and phrases are used and ideas are not expressed with clarity.	Errors in grammar and usage create confusion of meaning.
0	The response demonstrates no evidence of the ability to write an informative essay.			

TASK 3 RESPONSE TO LITERATURE

Page 181

1. d.

2. Prose Constructed-Response

Scoring Notes: Use the rubric to evaluate student responses. Responses may include but are limited to:

- Evidence that Helen was captive within the city of Troy, and that Odysseus wants to take her back.

- Evidence that Athena appeared before Odysseus and told him to build a giant wooden horse, giving him a way to attack the Trojans inside the walls of the city.

2	The response gives sufficient evidence of the ability to gather, analyze, and integrate information within a source.
1	The response gives limited evidence of the ability to gather, analyze, and integrate information within a source.
0	The response provides no evidence of the ability to gather, analyze, and integrate information within a source.

3. Prose Constructed-Response

Scoring Notes: Use the rubric to evaluate student responses. Responses may include but are not limited to:

- Evidence that the captured Greek soldier settles the argument about what the wooden horse is and why it was left.

- Evidence that the captured Greek soldier pretends he is a traitor, in order to gain the Trojans' trust.

2	The response gives sufficient evidence of the ability to gather, analyze, and integrate information within a source.
1	The response gives limited evidence of the ability to gather, analyze, and integrate information within a source.
0	The response provides no evidence of the ability to gather, analyze, and integrate information within a source.

Page 182
Response to Literature

Scoring Notes: Use the rubric to evaluate student responses.

	Development of Ideas	Organization	Clarity of Language	Language and Conventions
4	The response addresses the prompt and shows effective and comprehensive development of the controlling idea using text-based evidence, clear and convincing reasoning, and/or description.	The response demonstrates coherence and clarity, a logical organization that includes an introduction and conclusion, and a logical progression of ideas.	The response establishes and maintains an effective style, including precise language, descriptive words and phrases, connecting words and phrases, and academic vocabulary.	The response demonstrates a command of standard English conventions consistent with effectively edited writing.

	Development of Ideas	Organization	Clarity of Language	Language and Conventions
3	The response addresses the prompt and shows effective development of the topic using text-based evidence, reasoning, and/or description.	The response demonstrates some logical organization and includes an introduction and conclusion.	Some descriptive words, as well as some connecting words and phrases, are used to express ideas with clarity.	The response demonstrates a command of standard English conventions, although there may be some minor errors in grammar and usage.
2	The response addresses the prompt and shows some development of the topic but fails to use text-based evidence, reasoning, and/or description.	The response demonstrates little logical organization and includes either an introduction or a conclusion.	Few descriptive words, as well as a few connecting words and phrases, are used and ideas are not expressed as clearly as possible.	The response demonstrates a command of standard English conventions, although there are major errors in grammar and usage.
1	The response does not directly address the prompt, shows no development of the topic, and fails to use text-based evidence, reasoning, and/or description.	The response demonstrates little logical organization and fails to include either an introduction or a conclusion.	No descriptive words or connecting words or phrases are used and ideas are not expressed with clarity.	Errors in grammar and usage create confusion of meaning.
0	The response demonstrates no evidence of the ability to write a response to literature.			

TASK 4 NARRATIVE

Page 191

1. b.

2. Prose Constructed-Response

Scoring Notes: Use the rubric to evaluate student responses. Responses may include but are not limited to:

- Evidence of challenges from sickness or lack of food and water.
- Evidence of challenges posed by damaged wagons that would require repair.
- Evidence of the passage being dangerous.

2	The response gives sufficient evidence of the ability to utilize factual information from multiple sources to support a narrative.
1	The response gives limited evidence of the ability to utilize factual information from multiple sources to support a narrative.
0	The response gives no evidence of the ability to support a narrative with factual information from multiple sources.

3. Prose Constructed-Response

Scoring Notes: Use the rubric to evaluate student responses. Responses may include but are not limited to:

- Evidence of the need for food, and the importance of packing food and equipment for cooking.
- Evidence of the need for shelter and warmth, and the importance of packing items like beds, blankets, and warm clothing.
- Evidence of the need to make repairs and do work, and the importance of packing tools.
- Evidence of the need for self defense, and the importance of packing weapons.

2	The response gives sufficient evidence of the ability to utilize factual information from multiple sources to support a narrative.
1	The response gives limited evidence of the ability to utilize factual information from multiple sources to support a narrative.
0	The response gives no evidence of the ability to support a narrative with factual information from multiple sources.

Page 192
Narrative

Scoring Notes: Use the rubric to evaluate student responses.

	Development of Ideas	Organization	Clarity of Language	Language and Conventions
4	The response addresses the prompt and effectively establishes a narrator, setting, and characters.	The response demonstrates coherence and clarity, a logical organization that includes an introduction and conclusion, and a logical progression of ideas.	The response establishes and maintains an effective style, including precise language, descriptive words and phrases, connecting words and phrases, and dialogue.	The response demonstrates a command of standard English conventions consistent with effectively edited writing.
3	The response addresses the prompt and adequately establishes a narrator, setting, and characters.	The response demonstrates some logical organization and includes an introduction and conclusion.	Some descriptive words, as well as some connecting words and phrases, are used to express ideas with clarity.	The response demonstrates a command of standard English conventions, although there may be some minor errors in grammar and usage.
2	The response addresses the prompt, but inconsistently establishes a narrator, setting, and characters.	The response demonstrates little logical organization and includes either an introduction or a conclusion.	Few descriptive words and few connecting words and phrases are used, and ideas are not expressed as clearly as possible.	The response demonstrates a command of standard English conventions, although there are major errors in grammar and usage.

	Development of Ideas	Organization	Clarity of Language	Language and Conventions
1	The response does not directly address the prompt. shows no development of the topic and fails to use text-based evidence, reasoning, and/or description.	The response demonstrates little logical organization and fails to include either an introduction or a conclusion.	No descriptive words or connecting words or phrases are used, and ideas are not expressed with clarity.	Errors in grammar and usage create confusion of meaning.
0	The response demonstrates no evidence of the ability to write a narrative.			